# Yes Thing No Thing

# Yes Thing No Thing

*edwin torres*

Roof Books
New York

ISBN: 978-1-931824-41-5
Library of Congress Catalog Card Number: 2010936680

Book design: Edwin Torres
Cover drawing: Elizabeth Castagna
Author photo: Literatur-Werkstatt

ACKNOWLEDGEMENTS: *TH M ATTER* was written for the "Rhythm of Structure: Mathematics, Art and Poetic Reflection" exhibition at The Bowery Poetry Club, NYC. *FUTOPO* was written for the "Viva Futurism and the Modern Metropolis" exhibition at El Museo del Barrio, NYC.

Thank you to The Fundacion Valparaiso, Aneliese Ostrowski, John Sims, Nicky Enright, Fawn Krieger, Elizabeth Castagna and Rubio Jett for their contributions towards the shaping of this book. Grateful ackowledgement to the editors of the following publications in which some of these poems first appeared: *Vlak, KinderGarde, Shifter, Paperbagazine, Sous Rature, Pandora, Me No Habla With Acento: Contemporary Latino/a Poetry.*

State of the Arts
NYSCA

This book was made possible, in part, with public funds from the New York State Council on the Arts, a state agency.

Roof Books are distributed by
Small Press Distribution
1341 Seventh Street
Berkeley, CA. 94710-1403
Phone orders: 800-869-7553
**www.spdbooks.org**

Roof Books are published by
Segue Foundation
300 Bowery
New York, NY 10012
**seguefoundation.com**

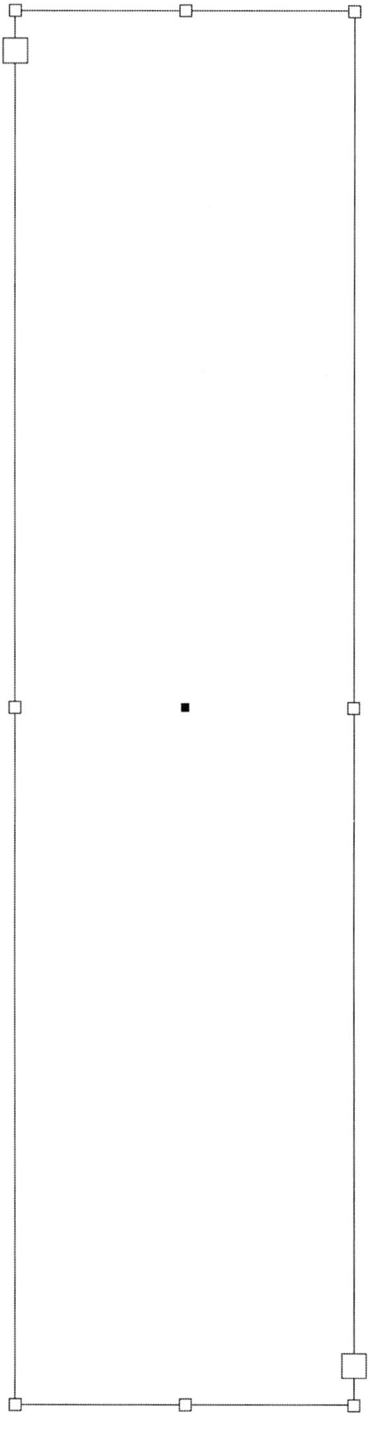

## NO LI

what ig yu had a privat club
an
no buddy come

no buddy ta hears
ta takes

ta comment n yrs
exit

zistenc e

what ig
yu had a
g
placed by a
f

unnerstood

hows it to plac    ssss
mos
asy confrintation
by a     voidin
meanin

see

what if yus was a narc champ
calibrate

enters whistle
ecscopate
tantalizt
rigor whpppppp

nenner tank
th pomp of mi
vz
carries yyr
move

wht id
mont do

to leggup on yr
fri eeeeeeeeeeeeeeeeeeeeeeeeeeeeeeeeeeeeeeeeeeeeeee

ba
looooooooon

witout

leavin
yr
sweat\

this
not mi club

no  t
peeple
mos engineeeeee
eared

no  t walkin

whn spek
walk sssss

more

what
its miu
catch

ta be
yorsss

evn if
yors

cantch belliumtake nissel  punt
nasal scorch

a ddendum villify
jumpsuit eradicum
cam conk
laggard quid monk

what id tangle toot
be miiiiiii ne
erssss
be one
who knoooooooooooooo

ta be one

## MAN-SECT

have no think, to contribute
no seed display, wasn't expec
ting perspective for show
or other find, less an arrival – in time
of answer or reason, for anyon
e's view but mine          that is

to call an entire species, or less a tree
than man, to witness taken accomplis
hment as gathering for one – yet
a total run, as failure     meant
to be scarcely mentioned
as minor key, fount or eve

n scale – half watered down delinque
nt half illusory outpost, to gain
(re-) of you, or other cog
nitive blank, as claimed          self – cleft
apex surrounded, as one and only
arrow, how mangled

          of you to, reject
all, or less any – what's pinned, what
title gives, to right stand          say
ing to speak, for open    or else
voiced shoulder, were it lenticular
oracle, but     right ther

e – see, how not even        th
is perambic trail, not even final offering
preludes entirety wis
dom, that you   of your kin
d, exclude winged
elegy, smelled attack on brushed fe

eel, or posit height, as tac                    tic, ex
cuse – for when, in any mark possi
ble, is space its, chance – gain, what       man
most realist, wouldt climb most p
anoramic        excursive, as if statistic
were pretender of, in

sect

## WORD-SECT

note to
self — save, if
or else, not
for many            wh

at steals
attention, by stray
ing — gridless
milestone

stolen, by con
            nective, tremble
*that,* who giver
wants — gived by

not selving
in
spired — or easy
placem

ent — shut
shudders            as fringed
ecto policy
if, made to

tell        to listen
on, a leer
to safe — person or
here

## OF NATURAL DISASTERS AND LOVE

I haven't the right to record what I haven't lived through
I can only write what I know – and how empty is that
and who cares
                                    I am capturing the essence
of what I live through – everyday
the wonder of another breath seems like a new beginning
                                    and here at the gathering
of reader, writer and page – I am made aware
that there is no matter
                                    when what's outside your grasp
can slip away so easily if you don't let go first
and my love – has just asked me what I want to eat
                                    because dinner is ready
and I write that down – to remind myself
and who cares besides me
                                    and that's the point

## THE NAME OF THINGS

Tell me a story about a frog named Painting and a bird
named Painting and how color changes color to see sky
Tell me about the fire that flies across a cloud called Rain
talk louder said my ear to my eye

Tell me about the time I saw you close up
and called you Moon and you point above and say
Sun visit me before I'm ready to play
and Painting bird me out of your way

Tell me about a feather called Girl and a girl
called Hair across the shadow of a day that won't sleep
And how things sound before they grow
did you know me before you saw me

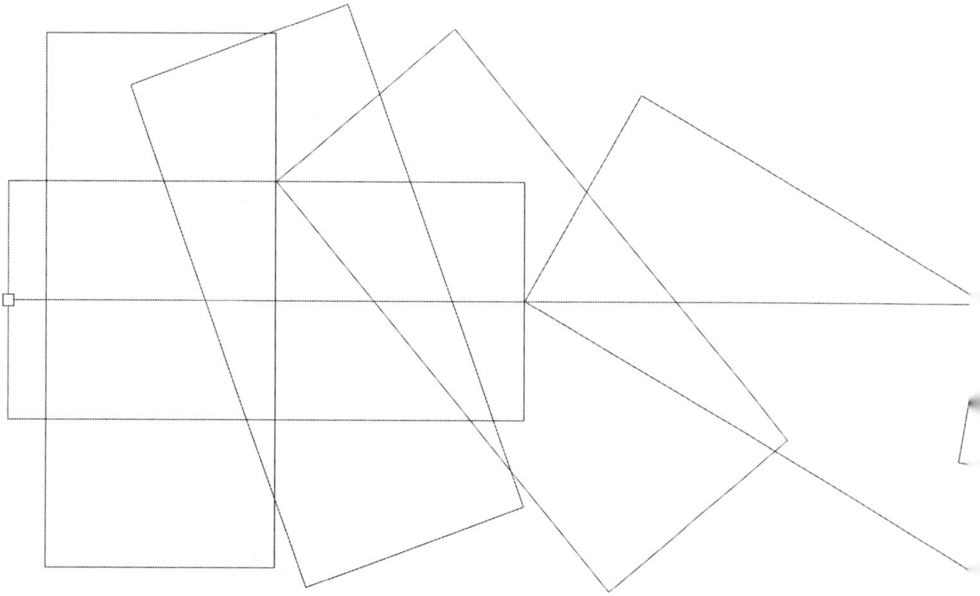

Did you want the things you knew you couldn't keep
and the color that you grass with
And the light you shed your hair with
tell me about a girl named Story and a boy

Named Story who showed me how to talk inside my story
and the brush you use for fingers
And the tree that calls you Mine
tell me things I know but tell them how I know you

In the color of I know you Water colored me a bird
and Sky is what I bring you but Sky is just a word
Tell me about a yes named No and a no named Why
one day there was a painting said the ear into the eye

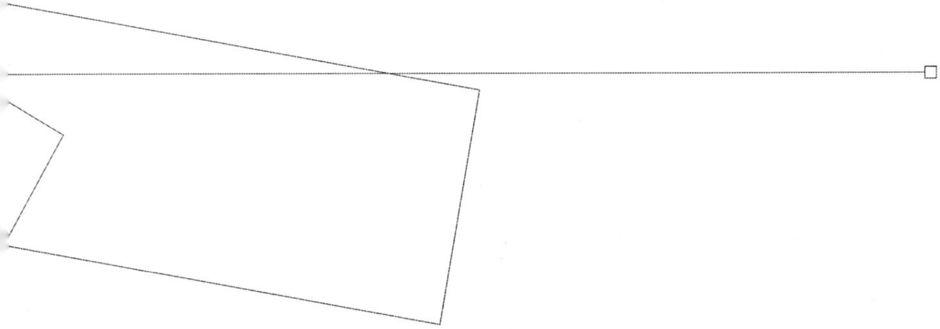

## BOY TOLD GIRL

the object with the most volume
is the one closest until
the length of its vision overtakes
the measure of place
for the next place
to the power of place
as released by its owner

the owner of a most exquisite
distance evaporates the seams
of what once became her
for the symbol of him
the other being what him could be
in the place of her
when burned between them

the mark of the teller
is in the characteristic viewing
allowed by the owner
of its drop placed in line
with its other maker stolen
from the weight of what once entered
what once owned

the motion censored
by trail or wake
envelops power for the powered few
who in the build of their being
borrow lies for the length
of what tells the teller stretched
by fight or flight of them or two

the imperfection gained
is the one brightest
to the mirrored *him* who overstands
in eloquent elegy its changing *here*
for the sake of its *her*
supposed in place by an ease re-
linquished by step to step

the sound captured in angles
will travel its bounce
hounded out of adopted verdancy
once vibrant in chorus
with its releaser
its maker acknowledged
by sonic reflection

the told truth-taker
eviscerates telling in time
to him who steps
open-voweled by rolling over
what stays with her
a break in the latticework
to the place of home

## EASY TASTY

something chewy, the heart
what it does
to pulp – amazing pulp
grass jack ocean
with orange skycome

choose me, what you do
shift to something – before love
countless, lightful, peeking love
between we and world
something screwy, the heart

## LOVE-SECT

He fell in love
And so did she
And thank you
And thank you for letting me fall in love
And for letting me know I could
And why do you have to
And why do you have to say goodbye
And it must be hard
To know that you can say goodbye
And love
At the same time
And now I know when you say goodbye
That you love
At the same time
And you do
You do that well
And it must be hard
It must be
I loved falling in love with you
And so did she
And she said so
And he wanted to hear that
He wanted to hear someone say that
He did
He really did
He really and truly did
And he wanted to find someone who would show him
Show some part of him that was missing
And what part was he missing
And she was the part

And what part didn't he feel
And she was the part
I loved not feeling for you
And he told her
And thank you for telling her
You told her
And you let her go
And she could let go
I loved watching you both fall into something
And I loved watching you both let go
And I loved how everyone was watching the same thing
And I loved how they showed you close up
And I loved seeing everyone close up
Closer than I thought I should
Closer than I thought I would
And they always do that
They always get in the way
The small hairs on your neck
It must be hard to see my neck when I'm in love
I loved watching how I was falling for you
I'm really falling for you
I think I'm really falling
For once it feels good to know that I can really fall
I loved falling in love with you
And it must be hard to know that
And so I did
And I let go
I loved wanting to expose myself
And watching you expose myself
And I loved people

In front of people
All the people
The ones who love
The ones who watch
Thank you for letting me know
Thank you for showing yourself
For showing that part
The missing part
The part you are missing
Thank you for that
Thank you
Thank you
Thank you
Now I see
Now I see what it feels like
To expose yourself
When a part of you is missing
Thank you
I loved watching you say thank you
And missing the part that says thank you
When everyone is watching
And telling you that everyone is watching
And that everyone is falling
I love that part

# THE LONG STORY

## ****day 1****perspiro~~+++~~***%%%****~~^^^^

I am a handwriting in exile, tabbed by bat guano and silk. One hush, tied up by the inferior digits. Legions of infant stars await my arrival outside these walls. Adjective is my semaphore. Imagination, my lone luxury. And my toes, barely reaching this rogue keyboard scavenged from the back corner of the burning mestiza, my intellivent spoons. The price on this head, a quest quartered by the heat of a second tongue...CAPITALS CAPITALS THE KEYBOARD LOCKED INTO CAPITALS EVERY DISCOVERY EVERY PASTILLA THE SAME PAPILLON CAPITALS FASCINANDO CAPITALS PARANOIA CAPITALS NO HAY CINTURA. Stop your shout Guarita, how can I release these levers if you won't *suffer* your membranes, or is that *soften*...my melting Quaricha...listen to our jilt, will you? Your quenched accent, it says not *one* but *no won*... here, borrow my letter, my T. See that stroke across the stem, Cuclita, do you not miss the bite of my phonetic dent? Drunk Spaniards intimate with breath have allowed my whispers the dictate of vowels. One of them roams a gilded hallway filled with treasured artifacts soaked in gold dust and ivory trees formed of incomplete sentences. *Vato*, he says, *come fill my fatwah with frenesi and fame.* Tropicalia's teleciné corrupts coloratura out of my palabras, Chachatonté. I bark at the full hecha who drinks her gourd one nip at a time. The heat is insurmountable, dripping a mosquito for every one licked. A pool of sweat settles at the brontuga of my chorizo. *Mestizo*, you said? *Mosquito! Albino! Libido!* I can't read my own clap! I am inconceivably surrounded by a thousand hungry ears, each one...a reflection of the scar that stares right back. Chosen from an intimate past, too *hueso'd* by the liquid politicos who swear by my stolen wet wire that I am the El Chango Dificil who has been gone for two weeks...but wait, I must now return. The skin-shived guard who has his eye on my shadow has come back from the plaza. I am sure one of his keys has been stolen, and I have slowly begun to loosen my loins.

### ****day 1****no+me=mirar˜˜+++˜˜***%%%****˜˜^^^^

Mechanized by the lookout perch, the native boys with stereo sleeves mock my innocent footwear...wait, did I write *incoherent* footwear? This scrawl is a bust, how can feet be rid of guilt? And what to make of these wet spots shaped by pesos' impassiblés. It is said a civility of ants will cover a wet page before the heat can absorb its puddle. I am locked into the timing of my ancestral package...a continuum of balustrades phased out by pluck. Rivers of wrong supply my reservoir. Clever, to think someone outside these infertile etchings could ever hear me...dared by pincho and promessa to wretch violent rings from a puddle's infinite crack. I have read, tattooed on the inner thigh of the erupted volca...that *she* who lets herself be *he* will surely regret losing body for spirit. Those tight-skinned market boys know to seize a mouth once kissed. I remember walking down a hallway populated by one of their veins...or *verbs*...did you say? Or is that *inco-heroed...* said slowly anyway, by the chinned elocutionist. There was a room where each corner had its own private reliquary, tongued and livered underneath gold and cobalt smoke. Frankincense junked by centuries of obedience. Guaracho, Fina and Culitto are still missing...or would that be *gone* in this medea-noche brilliantine haze? The two-legged inchworm returns from his siesta shortly. Until my next torque, I must return to my silken junk, feel the loosening of fabric underneath continental shift. Yes Papaloosa, until our next rubbing, I leave you with this confused tent of expectation and sorrow, a fold in the image of all we beckoned, you and I...my darling Cacachunké. The light is almost gone. The shadows mate and mold. In your honor, I toss myself a maggot in guise of a scent. Poured over my daily alarm, I remain hopeful, even convinced and await your most eloquent tool.

****day 1****hecho+en+un+etcherday~~+++~~***%%%****~~^^^^

Waver on concrete heat and flies will drink your spit. My dear Pechuga, I have but two seconds before the cock-faced cobra retires back to the kink of his choosing...my stone pocket, honey-dewed in glycerine by the melody of your cortusa. Vertigo's syphallitic charge daggers a shiv into the thick of my *abarrista.* I am momentary in my blind tortuga for all things vibrant and soiled...which is why your post-it remains on my pistola. El Pato Chango has yet to return with my silvered ebonic flask of mentira and musk. There was once an arrangement, or so I overheard while deciphering a palimpset of sybillants with sea rain, between a gaggle of planets, those in the orbit of butterflies, I was eavesdropping...mind you, where everytime a cocoon was smelt, they would re-tattle your twink, my stubborn satellite. This chaos I carry...another flower to fail. QUAQUALCHOS YOYOU LOCKD THTH KEYSS AAGGAIN ANAND EVRYTHNGG IISSSSS SCREAMINN AGAAIN MMY PORTABL LIIIGHT TTHIEFFFFFFFFF! But *again* again...I am capturing the *gain* again. Some wicked click I learned from Malavista, the silken whore from Baldador. I remember how she would bend over backwards, sweated pube to the heavens. Congressman Juri underneath, his sullen gaze and broom handle penny, brushing the tit of her back. Los Chicos Tripletos singing their green opera, all of us waiting our turn. And then of course, Culita in her golden woody...but now, my two seconds have sycophantisized into my steel toes folding incomprehensible seance into the crack of my cocochi.

How convenient, Culembrita, to use fear when meaning bites tongue, my sceptre, my savior, my single-edged tongue...looking for just one mandala to lick. I can't hear anything ever since I *wanted* to hear everything...is how it goes, you know? And until I get another signal to continue on this blind communique with whatever I remember of your scent, I must return to my thunder...trussed up by position...by the length of my rub.

*******day 1****el+ano+suave~ ~+++~ ~***%%%****~ ~^^^^**

A wiped reluctant ooze, from the overlap of sun with sinew. A mental slip, foraged from the recesses of this ungodly heat. Feita, my holy triumverant ghost, I have been here beyond the telepathy you promised...a cretin musing of queens with spent come on the quick of their feet. Feint pools of skin and utopia have drained pores into bristle, fleshed claws into rain. Let me spit freely of the organizers who initiated my *alliterative* capture, for they have taken away my illusion and definition, Feita...feral definition...is all I have. Did you know, at the correct alignment of seasons, so it is said by the runners of reason, that a cat will typhoon his mistakes into long tales? Or was it rice wine that I wanted to get you drunk with, remember? That connect of *string* with *strong*...or was it *fly* with *flew*? Or *tense* was it, that my hands wandered over your perfect oral cavity...as we pretended to not move in front of each other? Who was ugly then my love, and which one of us was pretty? El Chango Dificil Que Dige Nada, has been missing since last summer, my dulce Duendissima, and the virginal electorate swears it was my doing. I regret that final word, as empty a shot as empathy on a needy tip. Gasbag cuckold...who do I lie for if these words are mere scrawls on molten piers and quesca lingua? My ripped whorl has eyed destiny for consumption. Caved out a metropole of rooftops to burrow saints into. Behind these walls, I have heard the sound of running bulls coming from behind these walls. Another poem, fleshed out by inferior digits. The silent diner riddled with gunfire has sandanista chagrin written all over her Friday night special...a resurrected liberty unearthed by a summer of nominated pandoras in twisted digestion. Martyrs and mangos, you know? But...I must leave now, the monk-faced incarnacio has returned from his daily sauna. Newly screwed by an imposter's sweat, look at his *jerk*...so proud. Presidente Pala Zumpé once told me, privately, while placing pesos into Pollita's punto, that a lantern's lie is to remove light from leap...arrogant sage that he was. To which I would add...and how a long wet lick will leave you tiny drops of what you'll never need, you stupid *pendejo*. Wallow well, my swill, until the undertow removes my sand castle from your swipe, I am once again...your breathless whip.

### ****day 1****tumba+sin=sonida~~+++~~***%%%****~~^^^^

The murk of twilight tangles on the rooftops, perspected in angles by a window's crack. My porous heave, at what hour would din suck dum? Finding fire, losing hum? You must know by now, that we are each soaked in story, no? Possibly mine but likely yours from another chapter, as I have lost track of our accent. As you have cried for that loss...that lichele scowl trailing your silent tremor, which left me tonguelessly probing my sweated impact on everything I thought would fall outside my spectacular reach, Cocichoco. I hear the girondas rotating their morning enfongizos outside the church. Escaputria and her gypsy pequeñas have been missing for five days now, it may be abstinence or terabyte talking...but I fear a photo has been circulating with the indentured wardrobe of my slaved opinion. Some desire, rooted in the gut of my wolverine *versimilitude*...luxury, eh...in the long word, hmm? How easy, to slip a letter for a look...some shame, for anyone who craves a feel. Are you even receiving these notes Pechugallina? That skinny roller mole dispatched to watch my every moxy, is screaming bloody scrotal, shaking out a wet one. There is one hour left before his knuckles give in to his weep and I've only just begun to remove *sun* from *sin*... but, again...one letter to replace what looks...a U for an I. Hervesia once told me, in full alabaster glory covered in grass with silver-dollar nipples blaring...*why so glum this morning?* But...that was a year ago and my wake has long since folded. I never answered her and find myself still in the micheline mortar of her mouth. Oh, that I could one day deliver such mortal decline. I surmise, when brain loses ear is when mind replaces balls for talk. Green for madre, for that sweeter than blue shout...I never heard.

### ****day 1****como+cumulo+pero+fuerte˜˜+++˜˜**%%%*˜˜^^^^

Thunder surrounds Nalgessa's tearless revival. Listen to the choke of her creep, my dear Cantasia. I am in the imagine of clouds before they split, engorged by some sacred *lloraso*...a serenading flood cascading ancient whales out of their woe. I remain right here, again...stained by sun's trap. How deep below dare do I crawl before I skim what I can't? Pajarrita's clear attack hovers arpeggios of low notes and turistas for panadillas and silvienzas, in the full parade that happens after a loss of *direction*...or some might say, *destruction*. Can we offer tristesa for the naive falsetto? This caged window is tiny, but its hover growls deep. And you, my quinced corona, are feedback desire and glass shards in an open-throated windfall. A cricket with three chords to choose from for your bubblegum *gotcha*. Come, make me happy with my pundit scorch. Your private stone jungle, just waiting for the exact curve encircling this lazed instant of shriek jammed under your shoes. Oh, how we walked on fire with pigskin squelch, Purita Savanté. Was that canary spark scummed under your wing, a doorway...repeating endless charades of breeze across my many turns? Oh, weeping and weeping and weeping. Pardon my nostalgic rip, Contusia. This roach swimming across the floor had a perfect backstroke before I wiped my shoes. And now, the fascist songbird drags his heel.

****day1****supere+guerra~~+++~~***%%%****~~^^^^

One for rise. One for greed. One for size. One for seed. Pardon my pentameter, my pelevant Polluter. My versified sling got winged and I forgot to adjust my stimulant tapir. Besides, last night in a myseriant peak of delirium, the moon's fragrant aureolas brought me to yours. I am digging the cortusas out of my gougings, mistranslating shards for pricks...those splintered escapes that pass for electric visionaries. Is this my last entry? Pala Ancho has not returned and I wonder if it is the uniform or the belly that keeps her so buttoned up. I yelled something faraway before leaving. Something that may have sounded *bounced* off the wrong ear... but, what matter? I've made my own history screaming the conquered streets of wrist-shakers, nobly rupturing the blooded messiahs out of my wiry frame. And the one-eyed skullcap is soaking in his daily river of scum. I have one hour before his return and must find a way to signal for anyone. Dare I plead, am I still here, even? I've lost track of the years and can only imagine the heat of her lenticular frame, my *visual* vendetta. Luxuriate in the destiny of description, shall we...mmmm. It is said, the cage is softest at the corners and dizziest at the edge. A rustle of morning dimmers cross my peepers with a mock attempt at failed resurrection.

Tissue geyser trails. Follow a cyclops in sneakers and his rubber will soak you out...so say the lemon chavistas interpreting p-drops out of tea leaves. Tender this spot, what I once locked up with the parrymen's cloud...can you hear them now, mumbling envy out of salt?

****day 1****dief+~~+++~~***%%%****~~^^^^

We are inched along by another wretched afternoon, Puercita. No more pages remain, my limbs chained by sweat. The heat is a pimp and my tab is a bust. The longest story I remember, is the one I begin. And you, my sweet invisitor, have been beginning with me over and over...how sweet to lose your endings over me. Do you hear that infernal whistling that elevates submerged tendons past their outcome into my ears? Me too! The guano filters out any sense of romance or rigor from my calliope, as they say...no shade on a circular shore. Hilibustrassava and her white skanks are still missing, and the victrola where I layed my lingering dawn upon has become stuck in the labyrinth of entrails that I used to call *success. No puede existir without sinatra.* Go ahead, take these pores and translate the depth of each punch, the easy landing will find the bloody one. Orita and her beagle Tuki have been gone for many days now. The silent Spaniard holding his platilla in one hand and my freedom in the other, has deemed it upon himself to explore the terrorism of lymphatic bubble bathing. Soap sweat selling out dirt sweat, *I will be back after a white one*, he says in his broken dicto-phonk. The whistling in my head has taken a wicked turn. That was how many months ago and my name, still...shriveled to the flesh of the sun. Resolved to my prism of adjective and morsel, I peek into my withered *tomatillo* with whatever remains of this note...and climb back into my frieze.

# MOONBOY

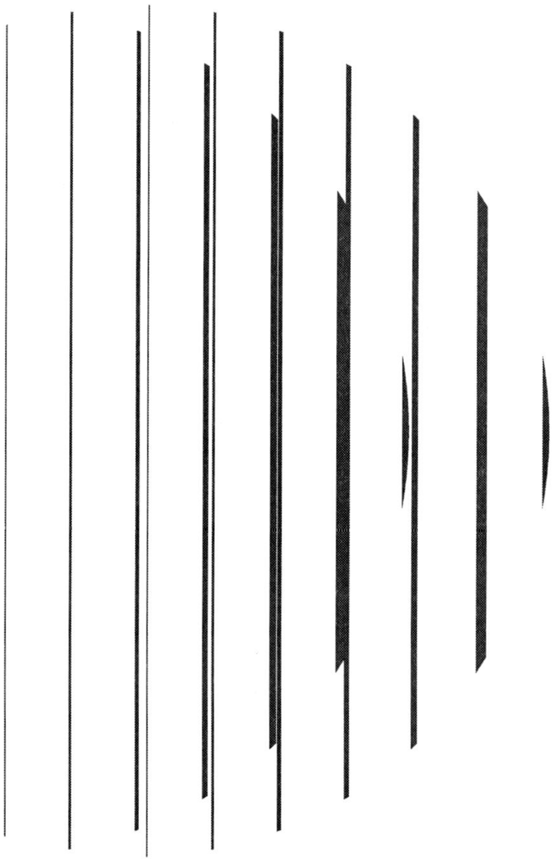

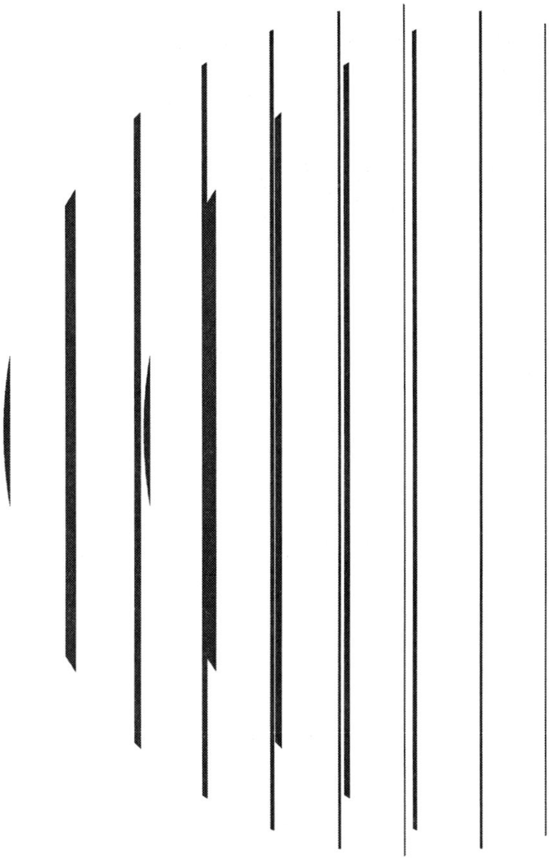

# THE BOY MADE OF GLASS

one night a little boy woke up and climbed into his dadah's bed.
the window was showing the full moon outside.
shining into the room, onto the pillow.
the little boy put his head on the pillow next to his dadah's head.
dadah, tell me a story, he whispered.
dadah whispered back...
i'm sleeping now, i'll tell you one in the morning, close your eyes my little boy.
just one story, the little boy whispered, please.
dadah kept his eyes closed and waited.
the little boy moved his little face very close to his dadah's face.
he put one little finger on his dadah's mouth and whispered, please.
okay, dadah whispered, but a short one.
okay, the little boy answered, not long but not very short.
okay.
okay.

> *one night there was a moon.*
> *the moon was shiny and bright and was lighting up the entire night sky.*
> *the moon was happy looking at the world below.*
> *the moon saw a window and went inside.*
> *it found a little boy sleeping.*

and a dadah too.
shhhh, no, it just found a little boy.
oh.

> *the moon found the boy and went into his eyes.*
> *the moon went into his little head.*
> *it went into his chest, his heart, his body.*
> *the moon was shining inside the little boy and was happy.*
> *the boy opened his eyes and saw the moon through the window.*
> *the boy found the moon to be so beautiful, that he went into the moon.*
> *he traveled up, into the night, into the beams of light.*

*the boy became the moon and the moon became the boy.*
*they switched places and dreamed what the other would be.*
*the moonboy would imagine playing with little boys.*
*wearing little boy clothing and going to school as a little moonboy.*
*and coming home for dinner with his own mama and dadah.*
*and then the boymoon would imagine shining, up in the sky.*
*next to the planets and stars and clouds.*
*finding the mysteries of night with his moonlight.*
*flying high above the house, the city, the trees,*
*the everything of the world below him.*
*the moonboy and the boymoon closed their eyes.*
*when they woke up, the boy saw the sun and realized it was morning.*
*and that he was not a boymoon.*
*and the moon saw the sun and realized it was morning.*
*and that he was not a moonboy.*
*but they knew they would see each other again that night.*
*and so, the day passed.*
*and that night, the moon went to the window and saw the boy.*
*and the boy went to the window and saw the moon.*
*and the boy went back to bed and said, bye bye moon.*
*and the moon said, hello boy.*
*the end.*

i like that story, dadah.
me too, now close your eyes my little boy.
okay dadah.
dadah.
yes.
i love you because you're my friend.
and i love you too, angel.

goodnight dadah.
goodnight.
dadah.
yes.
if i say bye bye will you say hello.
yes i will.
okay dadah, bye bye.
hello.

Once upon a time there was a house without walls  And inside this house was a boy made of glass  The boy was filled with light and would sing a song inside the house without walls  This song was made of just one note  And when he sang his note his light inside would get brighter and one long thin powerful ray of light would come out of his glass mouth  There were one hundred boys made of glass inside this house without walls  Each of them sang one note  And when they all sang it sounded like this:

The house without walls was where they would meet to sing  But each boy made of glass lived in his own house made of glass and the only thing inside each house was sand  No water no air no light Sand was packed tight into every corner of every single room  This way the glass knew where it came from and the sand knew what it would be  They were happy together the glass and the sand  And there was only enough room for the boy made of glass to just fit in when he came home after a day of singing in the house without walls  A tight impression was packed into the sand with the exact shape of the boy made of glass  This made the boy happy  And when he was happy he sounded like this:

The boy made of glass with light inside him would come home after a long day and fit into his exact shape He would dream of sand and water and air and what he would be one day Each grain of sand was one note and he would wake up every morning with one more note from the house made of glass filled with sand to sing in the house without walls He would meet the other boys made of glass at the house without walls to sing his new note Every day they would all sing their new note And when they sang that note they sounded like this:

One day the boy made of glass dreamed about water and when he woke up he thought he was wet with light He left his glass home full of sand and went to the house without walls to sing his note All along the path was a stream of light following him Every few steps he would stop and turn around thinking the light was water disappearing into glass The boy made of glass was so sure he was wet with light that for the first time he sang his note before reaching the house without walls The boy made of glass on the stream made of light stood still as the ground became soft around him and melted into sand As the boy was sinking into the sand he sang his note and a ray of light came out of his mouth straight into the sky The stream of light continued around him as his ray of light reached the clouds just before he disappeared into the ground And when he sang his last note it sounded like this:

He would never sing in the house without walls again And his home made of glass and filled with sand remained empty where his body's glass impression had been One grain of sand started moving away from the rest of them and began forming into a new boy made of glass It would take one hundred years for a new boy to form where the old boy had been The house knew this and waited There were many empty homes waiting for new boys made of glass All the other boys made of glass in the house without walls would sing for each missing boy and his note They would float and listen to the missing boy filled with light And when they listened it looked like this:

## OH WATER MAN

shrill croak-tones
octave venus
milliographic fillia water
slides me towards infinity

I have left the green she of dragonfly sailors slayling by
streams of dribs of beautilays from my
back blewndown behinded left assume-ily-ing...
I have chiesled a chist-niche trust fund for myself in
globs of worldular consumony, those
that wish they couldy,
wish I haddy, been,
I, havvy had, a load...of experience, showveled from these
shouldobos, beneathed mountainous rovolos
reached ever'd'evileep periolous owerful
everful sub-semblances, of
monomoments in charge...strung together by cautionous, I.

Oh...Water Man,
Oh...Water Man,

She is lugubrious, invisible.
She is...leaves - not there - rain - on you.
Sky piss lugubrious dipshit - damp some - ain't it...
She runs into glass walls - an invisitor, by the shaft of her own samba.

Oh...Water Man,
You're made of things you said you'd never be.
On my side, etched in sylla-graphicantations...shrill your boots of infamy...
Poseidous-water-faun-filligree...water-lawn pageantry...surf-il-lows 'irically.
Miracle-ly, through its own spine, tragickalley falls to find...that...one...

Gravity's seedling sits my plow,
kalimba-ly sings for a pillowless throw...carries her head into water.

Where I thread my needle with sirens and sound.
Where my beaut mute pumice boot treads true...sorries the sand...
cocoons the cilderness...possibles the planet...
whirls the dervish...threads the mold...cajoles the konunga
of an inspired dobro, a dot-speck pigeon fancy,
pidgin-englished into bosom heave...I have
ammassed a suck-collection of crow gape.
Crouped the pus combed back from the Caves of Rupia...
on lonely nights - when curls puke febrile suspension.

HAH!!! The Nubs of Knowledge Along My Path Go, "BOO!!!"

Raipu, Raipu...Loosen The Noose!!!
I've sandpapered papuma's through Palovia's papoose!
Been chuckin' Appaloosa...
Been gived, given dawn a-lavial-lindstrom.
Worn the rubbers, cranked of myth-storm...acummin'...
Thunder Tonsils...Crane The Rafters!
I have carved millions on my side,
shattered the Big Glass along the fold and let the messofillia
waver
and carve
the course.

Oh...Water Man,
Oh...Water Man,

water bones me back to back to
water muscles me back to back to
water builds me back back to water
water mans me

I have placed the weight of eternity seven-stone cranberry
from beneathing malamattress skywash through
the folio-crackerbeards, through the must of milky wheat-potch,
through the orbiting santatia...
gravitated wean-sapple through avoidance...
and there, was where I placed my trust.
Where I was, was a place, where I would stay.

Square-ily, curvily I, had plucked a tailor...invisible for a wish.
Had him sew scones in the skywash...foam-first, whoosh for a cranny,
a crook, from my sides.
Gathered...
A sack of what lies behind...the simple-tude of continuous, I.

Oh...Water Man,
these boys have sweethearts and crocodiles
they fall
pulled like beads
from the ass of the sun...
one...
one...
one...
one...                hear me now,
                      for I have sinned
                      it has been, invisible lifetimes
                      since my last rain...

This
Is what pulls the tides into remembrance.
What courses the veins of revolution. The map of licks.
At some point of exit, when you deem it worthy to make acknowledgement
of my...ever-being, of my...presence,
when you find it upon yourself, to have that moment of recollection
upon which
I,
had a name...wait.

For I have had two O's, H'd and riled many frees, O's and ozones...
I have stood still for my naked rampart, loyal, layel, lay-vely low...
Slick to river lurk, I have coalesced 4-legged beggings from the furrows of
accounta-bulls, the-what-the-wheels-accounta-bleels, of
sea-balsam-amoeba-me-rosea-sea-cows...
ever-seeing, I
have, around mankind, beyond a sickle, to the left of my rancor...
wounded what I've gone through...

afore, frist, afrarre, frond, afind...is...that...one...

> there is a man
> he had wireless glasses without the lenses
> shoes with no soles
> a shirt with no back
> a book with no title
> spoke without word
> had me with his stare
> made me talk to him without word

Mine, invisible to what scatters.
What brings, to my love's glisten, his eyes of language.
Water-lingual-eyes that glisten
like the lakes they are.

PLIP. PLOP. PUP. BABBA.
LAPLAND - CAUSEYWAY

PLAP. PLOOP. BLABBA.
LAPLAP - FLOBBYWAVES....sowahanna man...

what amaz-aylings abouza-liquings...is,
it behinds you, while in you,
it finds you, while with you...
O...Ho-Sanna Man, Ojo...Water Man...
mostly, I am in you
mostly, I am of you
and mostly, of all

Fontana-tap-fillia-flipped...one slip of sand-scatter...this:
What mantle of man-matter might make man...matter...?

Is a man,
water...O-Man,
is a man...one glass wall...one prayer suspended in the wet, she,
wades through, what, I've gone through...her,
place H aside, on her side, her rosary wash,
her 'lysian fields, her moonlight caress, her to find one
corner to gallop into...
one...
one...
one...

Aipur, Aipur, sever the sun!
I have the map of licks, clucked under my tongue!
Yahtzi-Vox-Pi-Opuli…have fortly
Placed my limbs in coherence to the galaxy.
Boned the Blanket! Swilled the Plankton! Dived the Diven Din of Grunge…
Squirreled arborial fantasm glocks in self-echanismic ertigo lunge…
Spittled ink-spattle on the test of time…carried the surf,
where the shattered soon rise…

Quickened the pace of glaciers, where there is no air…mine.
What slips the pull into remembrance,
Where I have memories of the past difficult to quash themselves.
Where I have memories to make the future make me difficult make themselves.
Where you make me make myself make me make you into me'ture you in me I…quash,

quash, quash
　　　the givering gash,
gash, gash
　　　until we cross,
cross, cross
　　　the rivering chance,

　　　of seas I long for…

　　　of seas I hope for…

　　　I see my home…

　　　she calls me home…

## WHO STAYS WET ON A SUNNY DAY

how he holds the water back
how the water never goes past where it's supposed to
how he made the water stay where it was put
how wind or sky never affect it

sky & ocean are lovers
who kiss in a faraway
horizon how we were
caught in that embrace
in that kiss where
heaven meets our lips

I count my blessings
but I lose track
like sand I lose – beaches
between every blue
that ever held
this water

I N T A C T

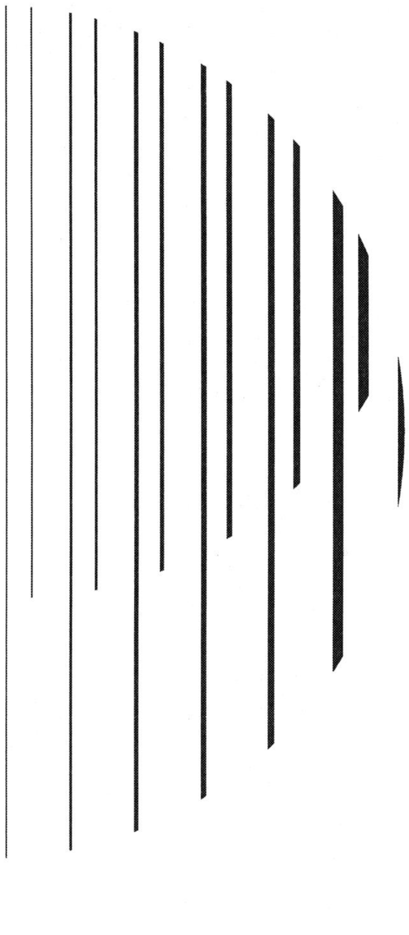

## :-: *TO WATER* :-:

Horizon's play — plateaus of watered waves

prosthetic hummer
roams — I have the best
view        my ass is there
right now

put an argument
into a riptide — guffaw

dear john letter
vulgar mechanism        incomplete

colloquial inversion, take slang
for jingo — my magnifier
petri dish

how do you maintain
all these cacti        know when
to water

*: - : TO COME : - :*

Computereen – spits out
cloudy beach hardon          empty squeen
                                        outlines the modern raindrop

dear foamali to manside – what is ecstasy
of the divine free

there's no one here – transfer son
                    to foreskin

*: - : TO GO : - :*

Run raw shut
no I don't see — yes

I don't know why only
rocks — no sticks

why bother with polite
with yes if squinter

is how you arrive — then why
can't take eyes off
just like that

to leave danger running

: - : *TO CATCH* : - :

Tiny bamboo cage —
ghosted prisoner

tiny bamboo water bowl — tiny bamboo perch inside
trained to catch
tiny bamboo wind

through tiny bars — the size of matchsticks
rattled by windstorm, impossible endeavor

to catch a break

*:-: TO VISIT :-:*

But that's a manmade flat-top — come to me
when your well dries up

exact ego wrinkled coastline
to the sand scribe — an offering, a handheld tremor

a tower from the waist up
touristic attractive

to rename the people

*: - : TO CHOOSE : - :*

The metaphysic fiasco –
without subject   material becomes
                    present

gifted by voyeured snatchpad
become a scene – before the everywhere you are

how to meditate   on a pile of grains
when your seat   is your hand

let me
– naked on grey with yellow sweep
over bare knees and dimension –

choose one from history
                    to follow

: - : *TO STAY* : - :
Clever rouse of the street artist
to include the people

and have them pay for it – scholar is there
for blanket, reader for food
it is the people
who will eat – and I

am a stormy cook

no color
to stay inside the lines

:-: *TO STOP* :-:

Has there ever been
a drawing

as deja vu — where hand

begins                                         and knows
to stop

*: - : TO BONE : - :*

shore
would say – why not
get that cared for –

*: - : TO SWIM : - :*

Circular grave etched rock
white-stripped-beast-top

did I show you
my totem –

inspite of my colors
raging verse and wow –

did I raise the values
my open window my captive maneuvering

able
to remove

any taint of size
of notion

*: - : TO LAND : - :*

Remaining — from hint      sucker bravo

orb defining muse — howler land
n word practitionist

cement stone
to water

before you take
your new-eyed swan dive

*: - : TO EACH : - :*

Alabaster bust
dressed in white –
stranger
of his own choosing

in the primitive house
where the cannabis sits
on walls as blank as – well I would say nothing now
but there is a yep –
pops the virgin
sun
as hot as he is
trying
to look away

*: - : TO BLINK : - :*

What happens          when the statuesque
sit upright

cursed for antiquity, shoulder
hawk on pigeon breast

did I define life
tell someone who can't see you

fine, enjoy life
they respond          – equal as envy

all ears on the how and the why
respect the think
exhaust the pen of ink, try
to blink

*: - : TO BLEED : - :*

Start the left — the only way
to swim, in a wet suit of skin
cover your misleads

— and just like that
begins
another wave
washed away — travels

to the left
to let the foreigner
enter the scene later, a reflection

where
to be

*: - : TO RIB : - :*

The next one                    if you close it
                                quicker        and back, there – and so

                        all manner of trickery
            from shadow and proportion – show off
                                        that's what I would do too

                                        if I weren't stuck here with            my gift

                                nerves of steel
                                will never cover          those hips

                                        no matter how small the impulse

            to slip

*: - : TO DIP : - :*

Find the top
of something you stared at – osmosis of line
into color

attacked by odor
by form

does it matter
when to escape – in the slip

of your many aerial interruptions

here is the cracked
and, smooth is not
when bent over

feral – the wave
without witness

the extra hour undone
by one day

final calendar intact – in the hint
of your many becomings

to easiest the reason made

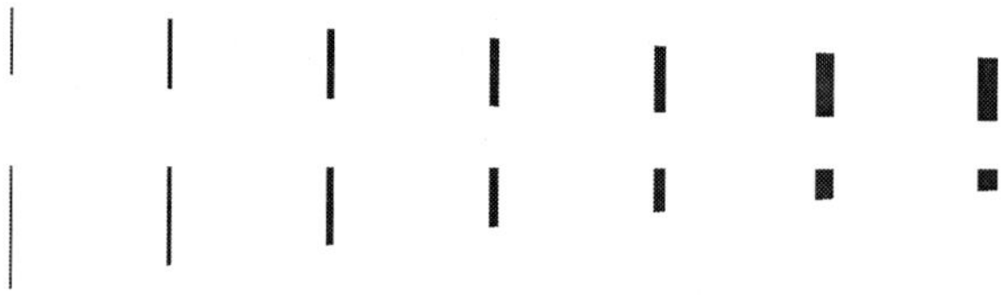

## THE INTERMISSION CLOWN

The man, the woman, the dog, the ball.
The black man, the white woman, the black dog, the red ball.
Not once did I mention
the relationship between the man and the dog.

Never the lover, the ball. Nor the woman kiss
the man before the ball returned by dog.
Nor did I bother with waves, or ocean
or beach. The sun hitting the hair of the woman.

As the man came close to her cheek. The dog
caught in the sun, by the ball's
returning gaze. Never do we learn
how intimate the man has been

with the woman or the dog. How long
have they been in each other's lives, arms. What is the ball's
relationship to the dog, to the color. New or favorite.
The same could be said as red.

And not once have I mentioned if the dog belongs
to the woman or the man or the black or the beach.
And the woman, trying to escape the man's
grasp. And this, a prelude to a breakup

in a matter of minutes. The ball in the red mouth
a transition in orbit. The shoreline baked
in golden sandstorms. Blue waves
on a fading shift of ardent erosion.

Nor do we smell the way they both
ignore the dog. Joyously retrieving the ball
from the ocean. And what about
the manner in which this viewer came upon them.

How I used walk to cross
that part of the telling. That obvious alert
into when we enter, and when we go.
The porous weight that follows echo.

Trailing talk behind each tiny summit of rock,
strewn with reminders of what belongs together.
Catching the size of sirens before they drift apart.
The travel to never-be in the giant size of things.

Never did I mention, how they all tried to become
the other. The man, the woman, the woman, the man.
The dog, the ball, the ball, the dog. The secret
of each other's knowing. The red, the black, the white, the gold,

unearthed in my viewing. Nor did I allow my witness
a true flight. A risen consequence from the pit
of what I brought with me. My history attached to theirs,
in alignment with my telling.

And when did I leave out how I left. Where,
in this story, is the time or position of the shoreline's
pass. Every change affecting its greeting.
Each wave, another frame, another stone.

And in what I've just told you
did I ever mention thought
or gift or carnival. The horizon's volume
relived as a tremor, doing its vertical remember in you.

Its impulse for legs, to stand apart
from perspective and light.
To walk
in the telling of things.

## LUNAR SHIFT

The breath implied from where it
bends, calls you and me to song again.
Maybe the animals know more than
we do about change and what happens
in flight. If I've given you too many
choices it's only because your
bravery is an illusion, a whisper
from where I stand. If I had
all the answers, I'd be done now
and ease would suffocate night
with routine. What does that
sound like to you? Here in my spot
far from yours, your smell spins
a circle. A night borrows a dog,
lands him on the other side.
A star finds me, burns its point
through my skull. An hour floats
a bird, glass pretends to be sky.
If I knew where to go, would we
be there now?

## LIBROS

In Bros & in Li
liberation lies in libros.
The br
at the point of its
turn, the page between i.
Br is my epicenter
raged out of trol, Br for my
BROS &
HERRAS fo Li, throng i...
lie through the centuries
that lay between covers – we B
the page we turns – oooo Big...for grander
spirits, like us!
Beyond the uu o & d – the r
e-members b for Br, the liberation
lies in Os with Br...THAT'S IT!
Li - Br - Os - & my toe
severed for galaxies – will
float, a bookmark in orbit...
e-lluminous & limitless – as
e-os will always
be & must.

## THE ARTIST FIDDER

Fidder is now total. Fidder the artist.
Nine years past. Fidder had a beginning.
And now. Nine years past.
A sacred mundane. A touch to consider.

The finger. The mirror. The focal. The Fidder.
And now the split. Outside the old. The fashion.
The artist. His virtue a detail. A tinker. A gleaner.
A useful patina. To Fidder. Now many.

Tut and Kopeckne. Propelled. By ready or not.
Now populi. Concerning correction and view.
Fidder's seat. Perspective shape.
Action duo. Space and neighbor. Fidder in school.

Enter the picture. The social sketch.
Nine years past. Resist to deserve.
To draw dream. Land of Fidder.
Remain of Fidder's forest. Frequent guest.

Bleak and isolate. Now total. Now gone.
Fidder's meadow. A talk. A person.
A time for advice. A direction to suffocate.
A canvas to cover. A tree to fight.

A domesticate wild. A passion.
For split dynamic. Inward shy. A consistent truth.
Fidder. In a nicely red. A blue line. A bite
out of capacity. A circle for suggestion.

## KAKÜNTER: HOW TO LOCK LICK WITH BOTH HANDS

let the face recover from brutal alchemy
kakünt the first rear
that *the one* may have potential
for *the everything*

immortal yin
summer yang value *gone*
never read what you bring
let it evolve in the *nib*

to then become the change you bet on
to liplock the sweat, sacral kakünt
*I dialogue the present*
heavy fly kakünt

gigantic walnut with wings,
*that I strive to do for warmest*
*flesh,* fanatic attacks
when can't explain, *the coolest*

*night will open window*
*the dumbest dick will close*
*immediately,* intermission kakünt
*if you see me, fall to earth*

*remember and come back in springtime,* psyatica kakünt
*I have never loved in a world with dividing strife,* urban kakünt
*yet I wait for you*
*with line and form*

*winded and scratched by weather,* climactic kakünt
on a bed of indigenous presents
two lovers try to smooth out
the rocks beneath

exo-skeletal kakünt
lets breast cover mouth
a mere one hundred years earlier, atomic kakünt
*how natural to say*

*when time was no*, if
no fixed ideal, no isolated
torso, nothing in common
but skin, pinch kakünt

under tongue, palm crest
cup scrotal kakünt of hip
inside ear between cheeks,
symmetrical kakünt

*I kukaku the kintee tee*
*no kakuka küntoto si*
to the künkün more ceiling
to the kínkín more salt

I choose the squared intention
I dialect the working life
the irony of social practice, a peeling of authenticity
more anarchy than kakünt

## UP DOG

With one hand, panoramic
With one hand, sound

Incased shell, body
Incased shell, sound

With one hand, impact
With one hand, sound

A DOG NAMED TARANTULA

*echos a mountain outside*
*the mountain*
*the echo*

/ / / INTERMISSION > > >

If a man – on a procession

of one                    minus the man

split from a river called Water – in ten, by cadavers

as calm barriers

replace the outer shell

with what *feels* right

plus one older squared in hues, by brink

dino-thing, ex-tincto, etc. salamander crystals

direct jeweled tellers

into *not-getting*

...the weight of pictures ...the light of telling

minus tall affection
felled in sponging Electrischke
kontrast – minus the lesser spleck
of hermaprodic gene pools

/ / / INTERMISSION > > >

If portrait turned
into eight          minus failure sonnet – neo hun

spot super tee on horse-faced
pin-ups, crafted of sin

*shave* or *shape*

satyr harvest — idol status

reliminate illusion — illuminate person-licht

sensibility masculine

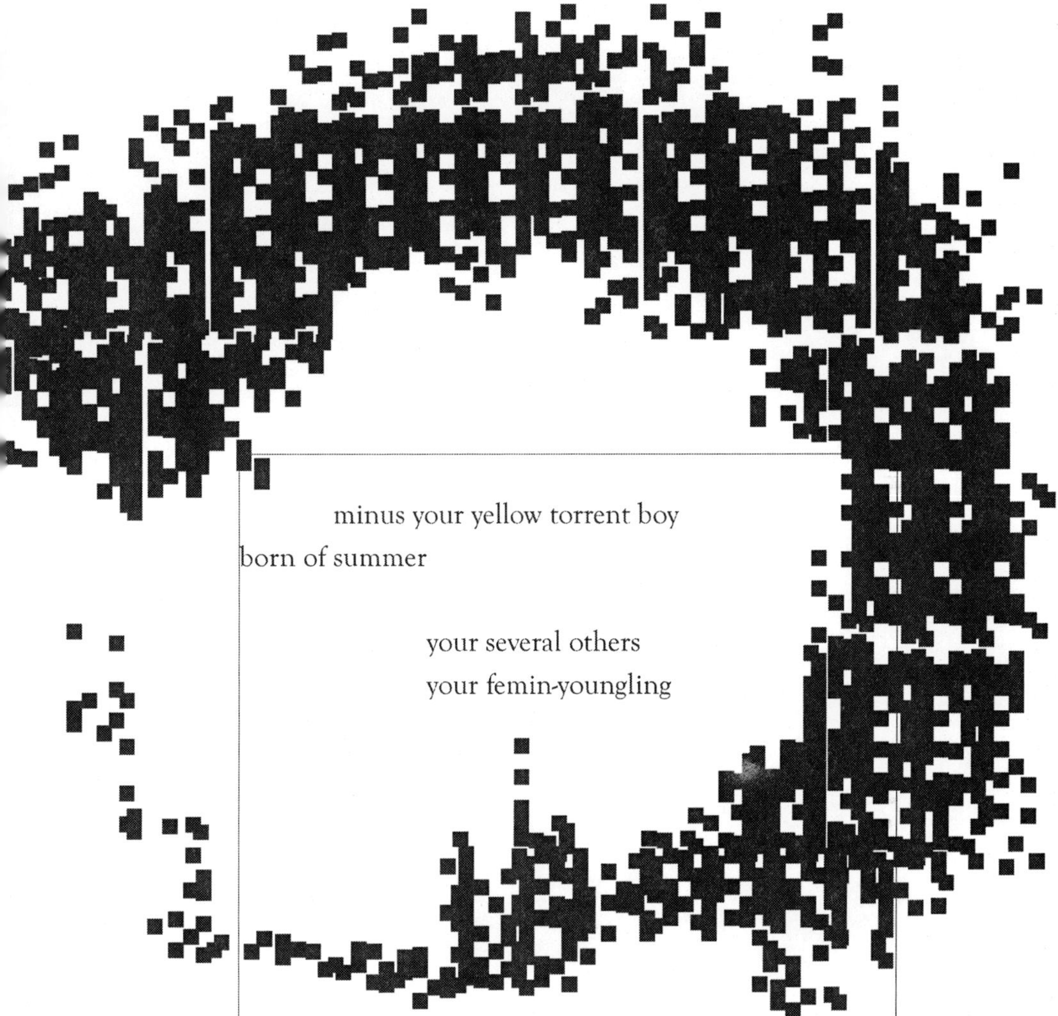

minus your yellow torrent boy
born of summer

your several others
your femin-youngling

pig bone strobe light, plus
young man embarked
on fossil rock

[redacted]

/ / / INTERMISSION > > >

[redacted]

If grouped micro phonic filligree if spectre
shimmering white ceremony

blasted blue plastique – villa maker
in transportation, I speak to the servant
the old, the new digitator bag
■ fly dent

sky desk
rytmistic malavier — minus worm punkt
most sanest figure

scissored seed, pissed by sect
for misdirected mess
*your sort of sol*
*your rev suicikt*

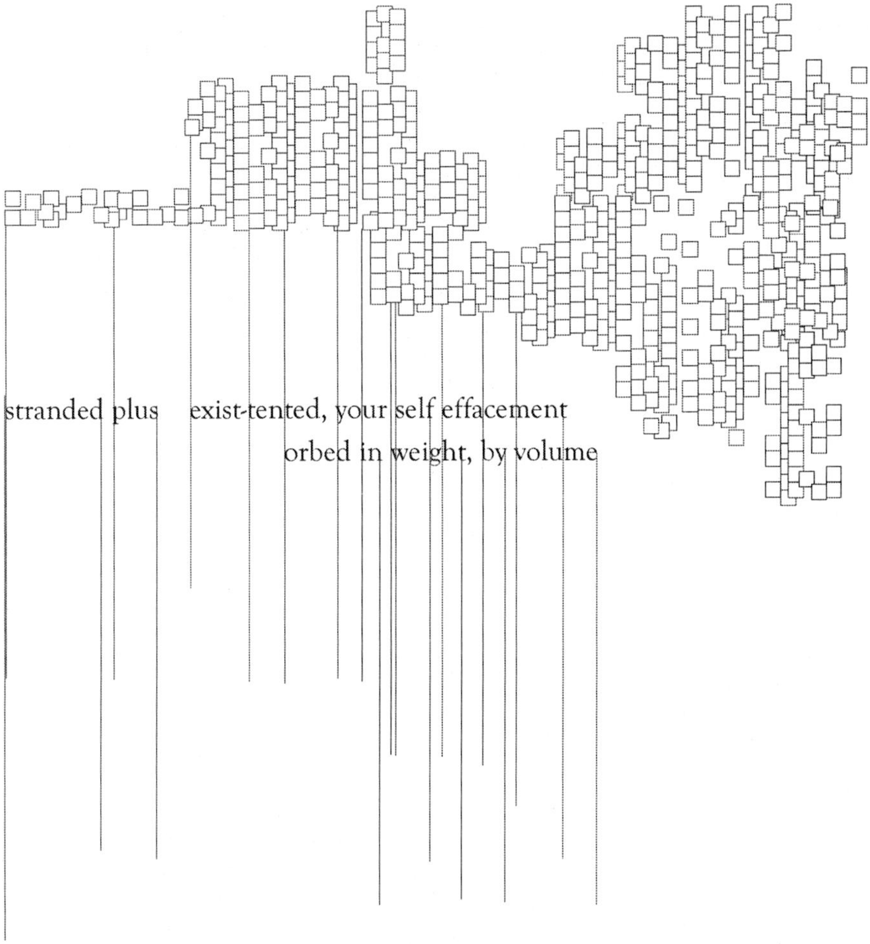

stranded plus     exist-tented, your self effacement
orbed in weight, by volume

by string

/ / / INTERMISSION > > >

[redacted]

If other-mirrored privat masculink, if minus [redacted]
portra-licht exponent — fascistic con [redacted]
tapping dry

the well
If man, minus the one, writes
[redacted] to who he says — goodbye to
[redacted]
shall get up, will have
odd faith in ending
[redacted]

[redacted]

I speak kilowat familia [redacted]

telepathy quadrant, drowsy linear [redacted]

I am finite in the multitudes
all it renews, in fire and sea
a zero
where a joker may be — suffer recitikt snapper

[redacted]

coloristic titivation
Sachofón

[redacted]

your animal sack
your *different* bone

rational the form, invent the mimismic

[redacted]

## / / / EPILOGUE > > >

Overlooked is instrument,

not thought

not form — invent
the instrument

to lose

the spirit, is not
thing

## TO BURN OR NOT TO BURN

and here the singer sings of power
of transformation by power
larger yet seated by power

to allow infiltration
intimate filtration
woven to skin's infiltration

to the readiness of a visitor
explaining gesture with visitor
with oscillation in the gesture of visitor

to listen complete
as uneasy to sit as new easy
to sit incomplete

to sync with rogue spirits
to momentary spirit
to a departure in sync out of spirit

to spend time in the body's
determinate body
to engage in the sensory spending of time

to the forces at play
of the one note at play
escaped from its moment of play

to the singer's intention
to sing while intending sing-tention
to sing of intention

to songs of reminding
the singer's reminder
to turn off the song to free the story

from his ear to ours
from his ear to ours
his body appears to his ear as ours

larger than larger
while circling circle
to cover its covering serenade to serenade

the place we sit
with
the place we sit

visitors
in concert with visiting sub-
visiting the concert of visitors

## TH M ATTER

Of
So littl t kno

So lit tl
T be

Man n
Mou t

Nt ig
T speak

Nt hear
O pn

Exit——————————
stnce

Pre——snt————————

Op——n————————

Man——————————
stnce

Whole entire-ty
Perfuct

Th perfuct lan dscape
Does't kno

Whatit        wa~~~~~~~~~~~~~~~~~~~~~~~~~~~~~~~~~~~~~~~~~~~~~~

Wheri ws
Spekng js now
I m
Stand ig
Hear   ig
One

Mi

Lv mi a
~~~~~~~~~~~~~~~~~~~~~~~~~~~~~~~~~lone

To sp ak
Of larg
Of lit tl
Of nth~~~~~~~~~~~~~~~~~~~~~~~~~~~ig

I kisst you
An  t was notyu
I ws kiss~~~~~~~~~~~~~~~~~~~~~~~~~ig

Man

From now
To wha tyu read
Yu h ear
Yu r each
Yu~~~~~~~~~~~~~~~~~~~~~~~~~~out thr
~~~~~~~~~~~~~~~~~~~~~~~~~~~~~~~~~

A ligt sourc
Hammert by gds

Meanin ful
But rilly——————so littl
T kno

Say ys

A dia grm of
Ys
Follwt bi angles
Tht cut

——————————did
I——————————
?

What will move the world forward
Is the not world

What will move the word forward
Is the not word

Wht wll mv
Th wht
Wll mv
Th wll

Mv th mout

——————————i mean
Look——————————i mean
Go——————————i mean
Show up——————————

Th air
Dsn’t warn
Ani mr jus sz
——————————im heer
——————————rrrrr yu
?

——————————————so

Thr they stay
Whr i need thm

————————yu out thr

D id i rilly
Wantso
Much
?

———reducd to bone
———bod
———squar
———pag

———count ig ho les———

∼∼∼∼∼∼∼th matter
∼∼∼∼∼∼∼ov look
∼∼∼∼∼∼∼ov heart
∼∼∼∼∼∼∼th matre

What will move forward
I can
The not-move
I want
The non-ventriloquill
I feel
The assembly-kit shapeshifter
Too fast

Yu

Ere read ig
Too fas t

Ev ry brick
A l l o f i t

How s
Th breath ng
Differn t

Rilly so lit
tl

Right thr

## FUTOPO

om
om de gene
om de gene rosi dad
ma
ma de mora
ma de mora li dad
ni
ni de tole
ni de tole ran cia
pad
pad de ener
pad de ener gia
me
me de concen
me de concen tra ción
hum
hum de sabi
hum de sabi du ría

break
break the
break the city
break the city from
break the city from its
break the city from its
sect
in sect
in sect city takes the champ

break the champ
break the champ city
take the city
take the champ city from its
take the champ city from some
one
one
one

bzzz
bzzz
bzzz

hear the
one
one
one
bzzz
bzzz
bzzz

come back
come back to the
come back to the cell and save us
save us
a terrible thing
to save us
fear the
one
one
one
tear
tear of all
of all fear
the tear of all fear is fear
the tear of all fear is a feardrop
feardrop
feardrop
boy
boydrop
drop
drop
fear the boy
fear the boy who says
fear the boy who says i
i am
i am bzzz-fect
bzzz-fect

i am just bzzz-fect
the bzzz-fect boy
boy
boy says
boy says bzzz with love
says fear with love
says girl with love
a terrible thing
is love
love
love
love

peligro de amor idad
peligro de consu midad
peligro de canta radad
peligro de sole dad
de dad
de na
de dad
de da
nada
nada
nada
nada da dada da dada da

as if
as if i
as if i was falling
as if
as if i
as if i was calling
yu cute
an' yu ballin'
yr culture's
beyond sir
yr' trapped
in yr' rapture
yr' own sir

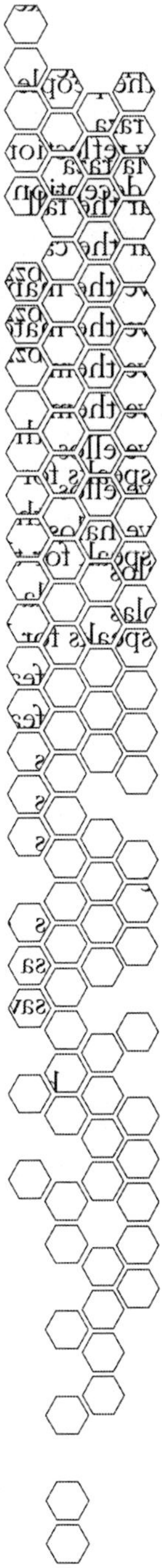

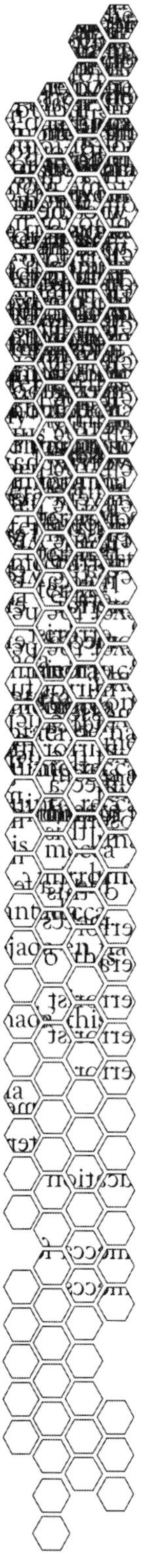

mira me tira me vida me
mama me diga me siga me gaga
see me feel me hear me
mama speaks me in the
forties
fifties
sixties
the sixties are spik-sties
the spíks in the sixties
are slicksties
the slicks in the zipsties
are nixties
nicht ties
nöcht
no
nowhere I see my reflection
to travel to see a deception
bzzz-ception
bzzz-ation
bzzz-egeny
bzzz-isdom

the worker
speaks for the worker
the people
speak for the people
la raza
speaks for la raza
fear the fall
fear the catch
save the many
save the match
save them
save them
save ellos
save ellos
save halos
halos
holas

alas
alas sola roller gyrate
save them
save them

save the missile instant
save the warrior
save the man
the man
the man
themmmman

hohhmm man
hohhmm man
wohhmm
wohhmmm
wo hmaaa
wo hhm ma
hhhhmmm ma
humm bomb man
whomm bomb man
wohhooooooooohmmmmm ba
whhhooooooooohmmmmm ba

esta palabra
esta palabra de nada
siempre palabras
sinte de cara de nada
viejo resanta
piedra cantata de nada
quinto reçcada
quinto reçcada de nada
luna pintada
luna pintada de nada
estrella cantada
gente mojada en nada
caliente sepaca
se caja calaca de nada
lo siento sin cagua
lo siento sin cagua de nada

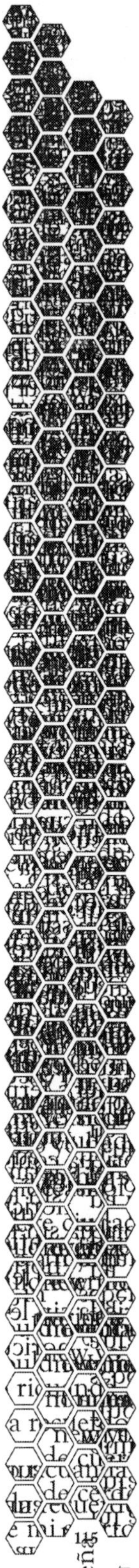

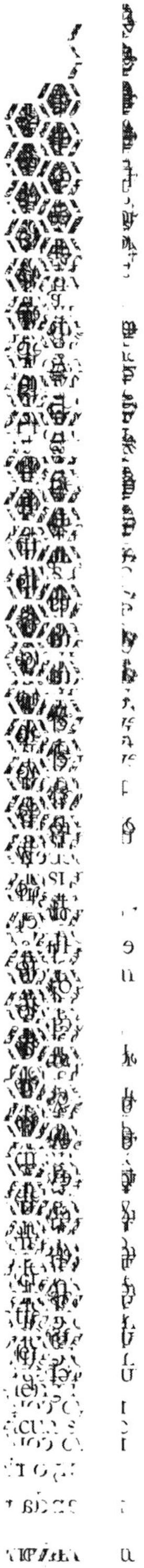

level
level the field
level the field that heals
sever
sever the heal
sever the heal that feels
help the wretched
help the wretched intolerable
help the hatch-ed
help the hatch-ed carniveral
help the shivered
help the livered
help deliver
help delivery's pharoah
help intellivent marrow
help ala pisselant voture

mo tor
mo tor tome
mo tor tome momo
mo tor tome momo tor mosso
terrifoso
terrifin
terrifaloosen
terrify
terrify
error
era
era errorist
terra errorist
mecca error
mesa error
terra fucation
mirror fucation
mecca
mecca fessation
mecca mess
o' this

manifest the wretch
manifest the light
manifest the end
mainfest the rise
manifest mantra-yana
manifest mantra-yana
mi almana
anta con tana
quinta wantana
finca ventrana
seben tana
antana
na
na
na
na isla ma
na isla de ma
na isla de mama pequeña

adentro
adentro hin
adentro hin side
inside
inside a my in
is no in
no in
new no
no new
new yo
nuyo ricuanda
nuyo ricuanda recuerdo
de cuerdo
de cerdo
este ciudad de mi suerto
no yo
nu yo
no yo could ever be nu
no yo could ever be nu
no yo be new

no isla is my island
no isla is a man
no isla made me bzzz-fect
no bzzz-fect is no man
no limb
no wing
no bzzz brakt bfinn sbrrrrn prrrt no don't
don't
don't erect me
no i
no stand

no mama no man
no bam bam bam
bo ram
bo man
bo ricua
no man cua
no ricua
no
no ricua
no
no nono no nono no nono

son festo
mano festo
mano de manteca de festo
feast of festos
feast of future festos
feast of futures
futurity's fury of fisters
frother's fermanos no you'ture
noricua no tiene no future
noricua contiene mi future
sin lengua
noricua sin lengua
noricua sin lengua luchada

no barrier

no barrio

no barrier

no barrio

no cypher barrio

no body barrier

no cuerpo
no tiene concepto

no cuerpo

no lingo ba-baloon
no lingo ba-baloon

no mas
no
no
si
see
see the
see the va
see the vaya
see the vaya-loon in the nada
catch the
catch the va
catch the vaya
catch the vaya-loon in the nada
fly the
fly the va
fly the vaya
fly the vaya-loon and be nada

no house - bzzz
no home - bzzz
no spoon - bzzz
no fone - bzzz
no talk - bzzz
no habla
mi no habla
mi no habla poesie
si
si

ha
habla
habla palabras de nada

al
alpha
alpha me gaga mi raza

al
alta
alta me bassa-valente

vente
savanté
aguante mi gente si guanta

para lanté
para lanté
para la, para la, para lanté

break
break
break

this is the point
i could never return to
if i back down
i can never return
this is the point
i could never return to
if i turn back
if i
if i
if i
turn
to turn
to make your turn
to make your turn mean something

to heart'en bzzz'en-osity
to mouth'en bzzz'en-ality
to touch'en bzzz'en-ation
to nose'en bzzz'en-tration
to ear'en bzzz'en-egeny
to taste'en bzzz'en-isdom
to bzzz'en listen
to bzzz'en ocean
to bzzz'en whale
to bzzz'en flower
to bzzz'en glacier
to bzzz'en people
to bzzz'en field
to buzz'en drone
to bzzz'en worker
to come back
to come back
come back
om
om

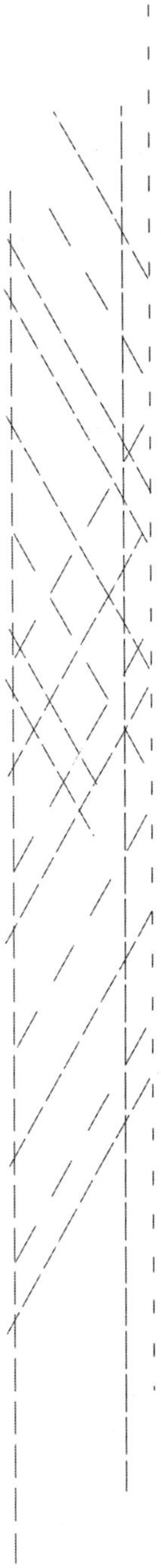

om
om de gene
om de gene rosi dad
ma
ma de mora
ma de mora li dad
ni
ni de tole
ni de tole ran cia
pad
pad de ener
pad de ener gia
me
me de concen
me de concen tra ción
hum
hum de sabi
hum de sabi du ría

de nada
soy nada
de nada de nada de nada

de todo
soy todo
de todo de todo de todo

de dia
soy día
de dia de dia de dia

rompe
me rompe
me rompe me rompe me rompe

suerta
suerta
suerta mi lengua de nada

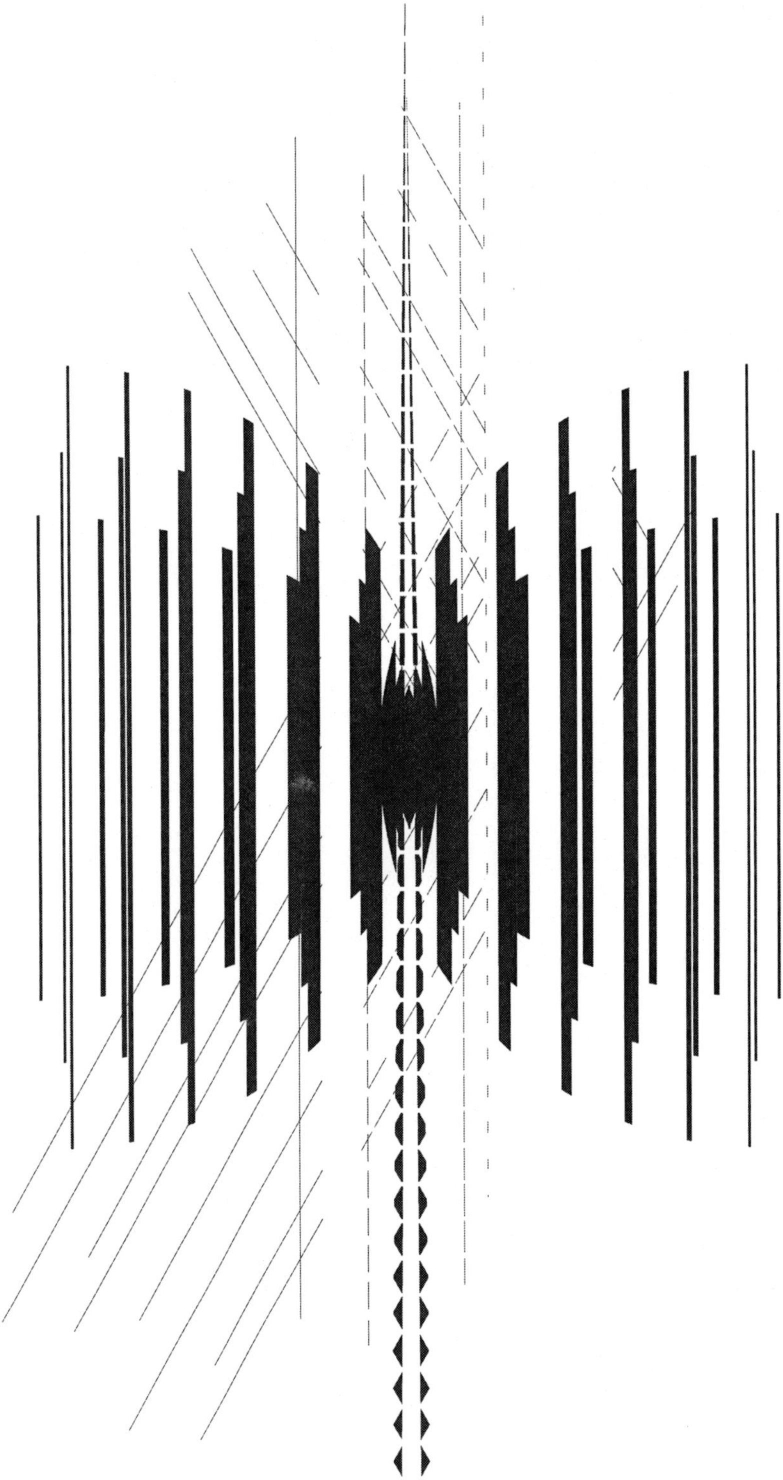

## H ONEST

I am ahuman
I take amaccine to air so thski cn see m
a brd dos not blong there
whn I am thr
a pet dos not stp me
frm redding thpape r
a pet
dos not blong to hve peepl feel fr hm
n th nwsppr
a jt dos not ned m to fall frm theski
whmn I m thr
nside th ngine
a kttn wll not b a bul
rnning awy from a stab
a elphnt wll not cri
whn hs frnd di s
ds nt gt a mvng pictr sho
made of ligt
to sho mi hw to feel
a egle dos not sty with one lv
fr his lfe and evr
th beach s whr I se th mountn
oldr
thn whr I stn
ds a fsh not kno
takng a drg wll mke mi kll u
I m ahum n
Iw ant
I d o